The Audacity to Heal

Apology
LETTERS

MIA ROSE DUNLAP

MYND MATTERS

To purchase books in bulk or for additional information, contact the publisher.

Mynd Matters Publishing
2690 Cobb Parkway SE
Ste A5-375
Smyrna, GA 30080
www.myndmatterspublishing.com

ISBN: 978-1-963874-53-2 (pbk)
ISBN: 978-1-963874-54-9 (hdcv)

FIRST EDITION

To you who are stagnant, stifled, or stymied without having received the apologies you've needed to heal and evolve...

To my little girl (the inner me) who needed these words long before I was able to provide them...

These letters, your words and mine, are the gifts that will keep on giving...

Contents

Contents

Introduction

I started writing apology letters for my own healing without knowing how important they would become to my own wellness, my wholeness. They were like a dose of medicine–unpalatable, yet necessary–and once I started writing them, I started seeing differently, feeling differently. The apologies began to spread throughout my body into crevices I didn't know needed them. I began to taste them, to feel them, to understand what I needed for my own healing. These letters are now a part of me, buried in my body, and the words roll off my tongue, spanning apology and love.

It would be easier not to write these apologies. Easier to pretend like the experiences didn't have an impact. It would be easier to be angry or worse, numb. But why "do easy" when healing is an option? Why do easy when I can do wholeness? Actually, I can do both ease and wholeness.

Even as the roles of those who owe me an apology have shifted, I still needed closure. I needed these words to be seen, or heard, or felt by me. So, I wrote them. Now, I invite you to do the same. Give yourself the closure you need…the closure you deserve.

Throughout this book, you will find prompts and space to write the letters you need, using my letters as examples to support you on your journey. You never have to share your letters with anyone, but if you'd like, you can. This is your journey, your work. Let your life be your favorite one. Let any harmful and toxic cycles stop with you. Release any confusion, pain, or resentment by putting everything on these pages and allowing yourself to begin a new cycle. One *you* choose. One *you* want. One moving you forward on your journey.

I took making it out of my circumstances seriously. Overcoming was my lifeline.

As you read through these apology letters and write your own, I hope you feel a sense of relief and satisfaction. I hope you stop longing for apologies from others and instead, fill yourself with all the love and affirmations you need.

Always remember, the wound may not be your fault, but the healing is your responsibility.

Part 1: From You to You

Apology to Your Body

Write an apology letter to the parts of your body that are, or once were, hard to love

A Letter to My Nose
To my broad, dark, chocolate, textured, and uneven nose—an apology letter

These are not judgment statements, they are truths. You are broad. That's the nice word I've been given to describe you. Not thin, not small, not petite, but broad and round and big. My big nose. I've pretended not to see you. I've not acknowledged you, even when I see you staring back at me in pictures. I've chosen to ignore you as if you're invisible. For that, I am sorry.

When others have spoken ill of you, I shrunk. Like that one time when one of the guys on the corner screamed out, "Your big nose ass," when you wouldn't speak to him. Or that other time when that tall boy was sliding down the slide yelling, "Damn, she black as hell with a big ass nose!" I contracted. I tried to make myself smaller. But their voices will not be the last I hear of you. They will not be the last to speak of you…their eyes won't be the last I see you through.

I have three pictures of you sitting right in front of me as I write this letter to you. I see you, baby. I see you. I notice you get rounder when I smile. And more crooked and uneven when I laugh. Like you're dancing. How sweet it is that my joy is your pleasure.

You rest a little lopsided, not perfectly symmetrical right on the dip of my top lip. The closer I look at you, the more I feel you. Even when I can't see you, I sense you. You exist as you. No requests. No fights. No pretense. Just as you. That truth expands me.

So, what do I see when I see you? When I really let myself look at you…

I imagine a place. A place before this one where I talked to God and said before I go Earthside give me a sweet chocolate complexion so I am an undeniable reflection of the depth of my ancestors. A reflection of their strength. A reflection of their light and boldness. So, when I see you, my chocolate, round, crooked nose, I see an answered prayer. I see the connection to my lineage. I know you are my bridge–distinct and broad and wide and dancing and bold and sturdy and visible. You connect me. You embolden me. You witness my life with me. I can be identified as part of a tribe because of you. I am me because of you.

If you could talk, I just wonder what you would say.

Signed,
The parts of me that have learned how to love you

Write a letter from a part of your body that has been hard to love.

....
....
....
....
....
....
....
....
....
....
....
....
....
....
....
....
....
....
....
....
....
....
....
....

If your body could talk, what would it say to you?

A Letter to My Younger Self

Dear Little Me,

I think of you so often that I already feel your presence, years before conception. You are your own before you are mine and I'm already grateful that you will choose me to give you life! Black girl, you are divine. A goddess of sorts. I felt helpless. I didn't protect you, Mia. I am sorry I didn't tell anyone about the thing that happened because I feared they would judge me. I didn't tell anyone about the things that happened I am sorry I didn't tell anyone about the things that happened because I feared they would judge me.

When Colin and Jay would call you burnt and tell you that your mom left you in the oven too long, I thought ignoring them would be more mature than giving you the tools to fight back or to protect yourself. I am sorry I didn't remind you to tell an adult so they could stop.

When I saw how you loved school and how much you wanted to be accepted by adults, I figured their words would be like water on a window pane and slide off or evaporate. But I see that it all still lives in your body. Right beneath your heart.

When they called you dirty and talked about how you wore Ashley's old clothes, I wish I could have given you money to buy some nice things from some of your fave stores—Banana Republic, Macy's, or Zara. You needed me and I waited to come to your rescue.

My promise to you is that I will prepare a place for you both in my home and in my heart to heal. I will give as much toward therapy as it takes. Both financially and emotionally. And I will stay on my healing journey and unlearn the structures that had us hating ourselves for so long and so badly. I was too dark, my butt was too big, my hair was too short and too nappy. But you, baby, are perfection!

I want a childhood for you that you stand tall in all the beingness that you are. You have my permission to fall apart and I promise to be a loving witness. You get to be unapologetic for being you–amazing you! You can let your guard down and love yourself and others fully now.

You are the definition of freedom. I want to be your springboard so that you can live a life YOU LOVE, a life filled with options, and where you feel safe to make mistakes, and to choose again. You, baby girl, get to paint your world any color you choose…and feel free to color outside the lines! A Black girl yet born. A fierce Black girl! The Audacity of a Black Girl.

Love,
Your Champion

Write a letter to or from your younger self.

....
....
....
....
....
....
....
....
....
....
....
....
....
....
....
....
....
....
....
....
....
....
....
....
....
....
....
....

What else do you owe YOU an apology for in this season?

Letters to Dreams & Things

Write an apology letter to or from a vision, dream, person, or an object you had to release so you could stay whole

Letters to Dreams You Let Die

Hey, you–

If I let myself speak from the crevice inside behind the tones under the tissues on the bottom right side of my belly, it would say grieve, baby, grieve.

No, it wasn't fair. It wasn't fair that I had to abandon part of myself to live. If I were betting on myself, what would be true? If I were connected to myself, what would be true? If I never had to abandon myself, what would be true?

If I shared my story raw and out loud, I'd have cameras in my home. I would make money from the story that tried to break me—the story that tried to bury me.

Instead of small events, I'd host conferences and retreats. If I weren't afraid and I was playing big, I would let myself be partnered with someone safe. I would be able to be hugged and held every day, just like I want and I'd let myself collapse into their arms.

If I wasn't caught between the stigma of being too much for one part of my life and not enough for the other area, I'd gather all the healers, all the leaders, and all the people who are container holders for other people, and I'd make space for them to scream and be held.

In fact, I'd manifest a team of angels to let me rest my head on their laps and grieve and let me have the funeral for the part of myself that I had to abandon at an early age—the part of myself that is no longer.

Signed,
Dreams, Wishes, and Manifestations

*Write an apology letter to the ideas, dreams, and visions
you laid to rest*

....
....
....
....
....
....
....
....
....
....
....
....
....
....
....
....
....
....
....
....
....
....
....
....
....
....

Write a letter to choices you regret, resent, or want to restore.

An Apology from My Bathroom Mirror

To the Girl They Called Ugly,

I saw you looking at me. I heard you mumble, "If you loved me, God, why didn't you make me pretty." You would look closely, turning left and right and twisting your face in different angles. You would squint and flip your bangs from side to side. You would take your glasses off and put them back on hoping that this time, the reflection would be different. I knew what you needed. I also knew what beauty meant to the world. There were levels. I saw you comparing yourself to the other dark skin girls in your school, wondering why they were dark but not teased like you were. I knew you looked to me as your only physical reflection. I was the only way you could see yourself at the time. But I had a filter you didn't know about. I filtered you through all the standards of beauty, you didn't pass the test. So, when I reflected your image, I showed you all you were not. I showed you all that didn't meet the status quo. I showed you...

- A nose too wide and too round to be beautiful
- A hue of skin too deep and too dark to shine
- A face smeared with large and small bumps
- Hair that was resistant even to perms

I showed you what didn't work about you. I showed you what the world wanted you to see.

If I could do it all over again, I would show 8-year-old you,

12 and 16-year-old you, 23 and 28-year-old you:

- The richness of your dark glow and chocolate skin. Chocolate poured from heaven into you like cement onto the ground. You represent the richness of Earth.

- The kinks in your hair bring you closest to your ancestors and more entangled with the love of humanity.

- Your nose has generational meaning and some of the most amazing women share it with you—round and buttoned and beautiful.

- The way you are…sparkly, gentle, and radiant.

- I would show you all the best parts of you at every stage of your life, at every single turn you take.

I am sorry I didn't.

I am sorry I jaded you and became your childhood bully along with others who pointed fingers at you. I am sorry.

When they called you dirty and said you were too black to be seen, you needed me and I didn't come to your rescue. You were dark, your butt was big, your hair was short and nappy. But you, baby, after all these years, I see you as perfection! There is only one you—and you are magical.

When you are triggered in adulthood by Ariyonna's stories, the four-year-old Black girl whose video went viral when she looked in the mirror and said, 'I'm so ugly,' I will remind you that you are safe. I will reflect to you the most incredible parts of yourself. You have my permission to fall apart and I promise to be a loving witness as you scream your way through. I promise not to pretend you aren't hurting. I promise to wrap you in my loving words and hold you there until you feel safe again.

Little Mia, if I could do it all over again, I would choose you and I would keep choosing you. You, baby girl, get to paint your world any color you choose…and feel free to color outside the lines!

All my love,
The Bathroom Mirror

Write a letter from something that left you wounded—physically emotionally, or otherwise.

Part 2: From People to You

write a letter
From someone
who still owes
you an apology

An Apology Letter from Someone Who has Passed Away

Dear Jeanrose (that's what she called me),

Don't you for a second think you are not still my pretty girl. When I saw you at the hospital for the very first time, I knew you were the baby of my wildest dreams. You have surpassed everything I could ever think of—Spelman? Backpacking for three months through Europe? Living in NYC for nearly 10 years? Publishing a book? Earning over 100k before 30? I couldn't have cooked that up if I wanted to. You exceeded all my expectations, baby.

I want to own up to something. I left you years before I died. I made you feel like you let me down. Like you owed me something. Like your money mattered more than you did. It was as if I was asking you to pay me back for all my years of being a grandmother to you. What a burden. I'm sorry I put that pressure on you.

When I found out you were traveling for a year, I felt furious inside. I called you immediately and said, "How you got fucking money to travel but won't send me money when I ask?" You replied, "Grandma, you use the money for weed and bingo—that's not how I want to spend my money." I told you, "I don't give fuck what I use it for. I'm not gone lie about it. Yes, I want weed. Shit."

I never got to tell you how ashamed I felt for not supporting you. I knew when we hung up the phone I'd just severed what was left of our relationship. You couldn't trust me to celebrate your highs with you.

I just remember when you were about ten years old and said, "I'm going to buy you a big house and all pretty furniture to go inside it." I wanted it now. I wanted it right now. But I understand now that you were always two paychecks away from poverty yourself. That you hadn't gotten out the clear yet. You hadn't gotten a house yet. You had one source of income and we all wanted to nibble from it. It wasn't fair to you and I'm sorry.

When I had my heart attack, you flew in the next day. When your mother and father couldn't attend your college graduation, you bought tickets and a hotel for your siblings and me to come celebrate you on your big day. You made sure we didn't have to spend a dime that whole weekend. I forgot to say thank you.

Thank you for taking care of yourself past the point that we knew how. Thank you for not giving us your last dime such that you would still struggle despite how incredibly hard you worked not to. Thank you for giving when you could and what you had to give. Thank you for not succumbing to the pressure. I know you have had to be strong your entire life. I know you are tired. I was, too. The problem was that I looked for my big break through you. That wasn't fair, and I'm sorry.

May you find a place to rest.

I'm resting in your love,
Grandma

Write a letter to or from someone who has passed away.

Dear Daughter,

I failed you. There are so many things I would change if I could.

First, you deserved a mother. I wasn't that. I birthed you but didn't nurture you. I have enough excuses to fill an ocean. Yet, I know I could have and should have been there for you.

Second, I hurt you—deeply. Physically, emotionally, and psychologically. When you needed stability and a safe place to land, I was stealing from you and cursing at you and not showing up for you during the most meaningful times. I'm sorry.

Third, I missed your childhood and so did you. You didn't get to fail and explore and be curious about the world.

You had to mother me...and them...and yourself...and bleed on other women because I didn't hold space for you.

I know there are still days where you are paralyzed in bed and won't leave the house for days. I'm sorry.

I'm writing this letter to wish you a Happy Mother's Day, Mia. I'm sorry you had to become a mom so young, albeit YOU WERE AN AMAZING ONE!

The cost was that you never got to be held. To know it was ok to fail. To need someone. I took that all away from you. Please allow me a fresh start and I'll go as slow as I need or as fast as we must.

And there's no requirement for you to say yes. It may not be perfect, but I promise I'll never stop trying.

Love,
The one who was unable to mother you well

*Write a letter from your parent(s) acknowledging things
that still need to be said.*

....
....
....
....
....
....
....
....
....
....
....
....
....
....
....
....
....
....
....
....
....
....
....
....
....
....
....

A Letter to My Mom

Dear Momma,

I am sorry you had such hard choices.

At fifteen, when you were pregnant, you chose life. At seventeen, when I was the little seed in your womb, you chose life. Three times after, you chose life again. You didn't have to choose us, but with a brave heart, you did.

And as life will do sometimes, it knocked you to your knees. But, like the warrior that lives within, you got up to fight each time it did. Even when you were too weak to fight, you fought back anyway. You fought back by making sure before you took your mental breaks, we had enough food in the house to last until you returned with more. You fought by making sure our clothes were cleaned for school or detergent was there for us to use. You fought back by calling the police that first time and actually pressing charges. I was proud of you.

You fought back each time you came back. You didn't have to, but you chose to. You fought back by going to rehab. When you didn't come to Spelman to see me graduate, I was heartbroken. I ~~wanted~~ needed you. Reality is, you could not be there.

Two years later, for the first time, you traveled to see me cross the stage in New York City for my master's degree.

You came when you could. There too, I needed you.

I am glad I am getting to know you—THIS YOU. Girl, you are a ball of fun! I'm so grateful you are here.

I was too young to understand your wounds, and you, perhaps, were too young to understand mine. But after having made a few mistakes of my own, I can read your narrative differently. You are a survivor. A warrior. A champion.

Lovingly,
Mia-Rose

Write a letter to your parents.

A Letter from My Lovers

To the woman we once loved,

This is from all of us–singularly and collectively. The men you've dated or loved or with whom you had romantic affinity. First, thank you. I have never met a person who let their light shine despite the calamity and debris around them. Thank you for not letting the darkness outside of you impact the light within you. You are, and we all agree on this–alchemic. You magically bring pleasure and ease and goodness and joy to every single room you enter and your scent of love lasts way after you've left. We all still smell it.

When I dated you, I was so surprised you chose me. I was surprised you'd be interested in me. I felt like a fraud. I couldn't see whatever you saw and I actually told you that, but you held on anyway. Thank you for loving me and I AM SORRY for allowing you to stay knowing I had no intention of living up to the version of me you saw in your head. I didn't have the tools, the mindset, or frankly the desire to be held accountable in that way. But I felt so much shame because you were in it. Like really in it.

I remember I came over and you had three boxes of my favorite cereal on the table–for no reason at all except #because. That's who you are and that's who you've been.

When I ghosted you after spending hours and hours on the phone and on Facetime for weeks, I woke up the love in you only not to have the courage to stay in it.

I am so damn sorry for being a coward in that way. You deserved better than that.

Collectively and individually, we love you and could have/ should have loved you way more if we had the capacity. We didn't.

We hope you are wrapped in the safety of love's arms with someone whose love is as deep and soulful and holy and wholesome and enveloping and as pure as yours.

Thank you,
The men who couldn't stay

Write a letter from former lovers, partners, and relationships where they take accountability for their actions.

....
....
....
....
....
....
....
....
....
....
....
....
....
....
....
....
....
....
....
....
....
....
....

Write a letter to someone where you offer any unspoken apologies or accountability.

....
....
....
....
....
....
....
....
....
....
....
....
....
....
....
....
....
....
....
....
....
....
....
....
....

A Letter from My Therapist

What I hear my therapist saying without saying it...

As you are. Right now. Who you are. Right now. What you are. Right now. Is absolutely enough. Your scars don't scare me. Your pain doesn't shake me. Your wounds don't offend me.

What happened to you, should never have happened. Ever. Period. I am so sorry it did. No, you did not need pain to make you stronger. No, you did not need heartbreak to make you wise. No, you did not need trauma to build your resilience. You didn't need or deserve any of that. It could have killed you and in many ways, it did. It killed and quieted parts of you.

The carefree part of you died and what replaced it is your need to scan every room immediately for psychological safety. You need to identify who the "bad guys" are, who the "nice ones" are, and where you will be accepted.

While that instinct can and has served you in the best ways, the learning was devastating. You did not deserve to learn how to read a room via devastations.

The trusting part of you diminished. I notice that there are very few people you trust with you. I know it was because you never felt safe at home...like you could trust someone to have your back. So now you move through the world being who you needed. You make sure you're someone people can trust. But, you are still wounded around trusting people with you…with your love and your vulnerability.

I want to remind you, just because this identity is what you've known, it's not who you are. The behaviors you can unlearn, your voice you can unearth, your authentic self—you can let yourself experience.

Love,
Someone who holds space for all parts of you

Write a letter from anyone else whose apology you still want/ need (former friend, estranged family member, etc.).

Part 3: Letters from Places

Letters to Cities

Ones you've loved, ones you've left, ones that birthed you, or ones that changed you

My Dear Zurich,

I know I said I came to Europe to write. This three-month backpacking trip was for me to find people who could tell me about their adversity, their pain. But I really want to write about myself and look for places to heal.

I'm sitting in the middle of Zurich, Switzerland staring into the night. I've written short notes on my phone, on pieces of napkins, and once even on my hand since I've started this journey. But I've not written like I imagined I would. Ugh, I don't want to leave this city without immersing myself in it. I haven't sat by the water streams or in the grass and let the sun and the sky watch me create my own streams of thought and stories through words on the page.

What's true is that I didn't come equipped with the stuff I need to write. I have an iPad but not a laptop. Actually, who am I kidding? I don't need a computer to do what I do. I guess I just haven't set the intention and time to write. I've gotten caught up a bit and haven't been following my "schedule."

For example, when I was in Paris a week ago, I woke up, looked at the time, calculated the time it was in the States and rolled back over. Then after a few hours into the day, I'd wonder what people were doing, if they were thinking about me and happy for me back home in Chicago and Brooklyn. I'd wonder if coming on this trip was something I had to do or if I was being selfish like my grandma said.

I remember her saying, "Heyyyyy, I don't want to hear about no damn trip to some place we can't even pronounce when you know I need money for Bingo and bills. Shit."

Another time, after I'd packed my two small bags and had my trip set, I overheard her say to herself, "Spending all that goddamn money to go play pretend." I froze. A voice inside my head urged me to leave while her voice felt like handcuffs. I am not even living in Chicago with her. I am living in New York.

I sometimes send her money when she asks for it. Usually between $20.00 - $50.00. She likely knew my traveling wouldn't give her the same access to the money. The more I considered what I should do, the handcuffs felt tighter. So, as I sit here in Zurich, I realize...

I haven't taken the handcuffs off. I have the key in my back pocket, but it's hard to reach. The handcuffs didn't come from her though, they were here long before she muttered those words to me. She has on a pair, too.

Switzerland, thank you for being a space for me to understand what is happening in me.

With adoration,
A traveler who loved meeting you

Write a letter to a place where you didn't stay long.

Dear Brooklyn,

I fell in love with you and then I left you. I'm sorry. I didn't know how much I'd love you when I first met you. I'm getting chills just thinking about you. Circa June 2010, I entered into your arms. I had no idea the ride we'd take together, the people you'd introduce me to, the possibilities I'd be exposed to, the communities I'd form, the lives I'd touch, or the love I'd create. It was an adventure.

Still wet behind the ears, I was a twenty-one-year-old Spelman College graduate craving a place to call home—in you.

I grew up in the housing projects of Chicago and had never had an apartment of my own. But this charming three flat brownstone walkup was mine—and Jamila's. But you know what I mean. It was my very own studio apartment with a shared kitchen that connected Jamilia's studio apartment to mine. We had our own bathrooms and separate entrances and space. We shared the kitchen and we shared salads. Yes, salads.

Remember when my mentor sent me a $3,000 check for the first and last month's rent and security deposit as a post-graduation gift. (My rent was $1,000 in downtown Brooklyn. Wow, crazy times!) He said, "You're going to need this." I did and didn't even know I did. I handed it right over to the landlord and saw my account drop to $156.32.

That's what I had until I got my first check from my first big job…three weeks later! So, J and I shared salads.

I slept on the floor on top of a pile of clothes until I could purchase my first bed and furniture set from Ikea. I was grateful. For a decade, I took up space on Duffield Street, across from the Manhattan Bridge and a short three-block walk to the Brooklyn Bridge.

For a decade I lived in that studio apartment. I watched the neighborhood morph just as I morphed. You were able to hold all my changes, Brooklyn. My starting salary was $56,500 as a teacher in Bedstuy and I left earning $130,000 over the decade as a principal, director of school culture, and leadership culture coach.

I became…I morphed….and you held me through all of the changes.

I called my mentor and said, "Remember I told you I'd pay you back? I can now." Without hesitation he responded, "I'm glad to hear that. Thank you, but that was a gift. Pay it forward."

Brooklyn, you introduced me to the first woman I ever fell in love with (outside of myself). She was a sweet surprise. A woman who'd cross an ocean for me and I for her– she easily became my favorite person on the planet. For years, we made life richer and deeper and intoxicating. We played and fought and laughed and cried and left and returned.

She was the first woman (maybe even person) I'd ever let love me and it brought up my deepest fears and greatest joys. That relationship was such a gift. So grateful for it.

Brooklyn, thank you for everything and more than anything—for her.

Signed,
A gal who misses the decade long love
story I made in Brooklyn

Write a letter to a place where you fell in love.

....
....
....
....
....
....
....
....
....
....
....
....
....
....
....
....
....
....
....
....
....
....
....
....
....

To my girl, former Chicagoan,

I'm so glad you lived here, even though I know you don't have many favorable memories of me. I know you have so many reasons to resent me and to never want to return. I am sorry for the chaos I brought you. I am so sorry for all that happened in this city in general and TO YOU. There are things you still want to bury—things you wish could be erased. I know, I get it, and I am sorry, Mia Rose.

Selfishly, I am so glad you were here (though I wish none of the traumatic experiences had happened). I can brag about you and how I watched you grow, and dare I say, I was even part of your transformation.

Can we, for a second, outline the amazingness that came from this city? Let's start with your siblings. You mothered them and loved them and cared for them with every fiber of your being. Even and especially as a little girl, you were their person–their hero. You loved loving them.

Your friendships—you have made the deepest and most wholesome and most transformational friendship in this city—*cough, cough*—Ashley Hall. Period. There are many more, AND that one single-handedly changed the trajectory of your life. The way her family took you under their wings, embraced you, enveloped you, made room for you without question, prayed for you, fed you, clothed you, paid for you, showed up for you—WOW. They remain your Angel family.

The project building 4500, Colman school, Ms. Straight, were all paths to lead you to the Dabney/Ware family what a life changing experience.

I could name so many people—Shalina, Idella, Hannah, Dr. Larry Hawkins, Ethan Michaeli, Sharon Tillman, Nan, Ora Myles Sheares) who invested in little you as you navigated the complexity of your childhood; Programs—Office of Special Programs at the University of Chicago, the Charles Hayes Center, After School Matters, Resident's Journal, Internship at Leak and Son's Funeral Home, Gwendolyn Brooks College Prep, CSBI: Chicago Summer Business Institute— the people in these programs POURED into you right here in this city— they are part of your experience in this city, too. Just because you're mad at me, don't forget about the love, the people, the light—more than one thing can be true at the same time.

Signed,
Chicago: a city I hope you come to love again

Write a letter to a place that nearly broke you.

Write a letter to a place where you stayed too long.

Part 4: Letters to and from Experiences

Letters from Experiences

what's an experience you wished turned out differently?

A Letter from Poverty

Dear first gen, aka, the one who "made it,"

Like a vulture, I swept down and swallowed you in my bill. I wanted you to suffer. I wanted you to feel my sting, my grip, my misery.

When your grandmother, a survivor of mental abuse, let your mother move in with your father at fourteen years old. When your father and his sibling were taken to foster care beginning when they were about seven years old. When your mother got pregnant with your oldest brother during her sophomore year of high school and her teachers didn't pursue her to stay in school. When your dad didn't finish school because he was trying to make money to take care of his son. When your parents conceived you as teenagers, I figured you would repeat the cycle and become a teen parent.

It didn't surprise me when your family moved into one of the roughest and poorest parts of Chicago, the Robert Taylor Projects. It didn't surprise me when you couldn't afford to go on field trips and you lied saying you didn't want to go. When your parents' drug addiction took over and you became their target. They needed you to say the right things whenever someone called or asked questions. They needed your savvy. They hated that they needed you. You hated being needed. It was all part of the cycle.

When you started going to church, I figured you would get lost in the dogma and religiosity of "the church."

That you would tithe, pray, and maintain the same habits you've been taught—God is going to fix it. It surprised me when you began to ask questions and not accept church jargon as something to repeat. You used religion as a parachute. It was as if you'd made a deal with it, "when I leap and boldly try to break this cycle, I need you to catch me if I fall." And you did. And it did.

It surprised me that you continued to defy your parents and run away from home when they punished you from church and school. I remember them saying, "That's all your ass wants to do is go to school or church. Go lay your ass down. You ain't going nowhere with that nasty ass attitude."

Another time I heard your mom say, "You think going to church is going to save you, huh? You gone end up right in hell." After you yelled back, "I'll see you there," you left for three days and attended every single class and completed every single assignment during your junior year. That's when I knew I wouldn't be able to keep you on my bill. You were fighting back with tools I hadn't anticipated. You attracted people into your life who saw how much I was trying to bury your talent, your voice, and your opportunities. But like shields, they stood between us.

How did you do it? How did you know to whom to listen? How did you quiet the noise of your circumstances enough to understand the whisper of your opportunities? Your family couldn't see what was available to them. How did you? I overwhelmed you with feeling unworthy and defeated. How did you learn to silence me? To suppress me?

While I want to apologize for my role in your life, while I get that you suffered and your family suffered, while I want to acknowledge the outrage you didn't get to express, I want you to know I still see you running from me.

Stop. I'm not chasing you anymore. That's my peace offering to you. Putting my cards on the table, I'm not pursuing you any longer. You don't have what I need to prevail. Instead of an apology, I am offering you freedom papers. You can live now. You can settle in and catch your breath. You're ok. You won't be able to save everyone, they have a journey of their own, and you cannot be responsible for them. However, your light, your flight, your ability to escape my gnaw will set so many others free.

I can hear you saying it's not fair that your family has had to suffer because of me—poverty. The truth is, I'm not here to destroy you but to make sure the "haves" keep having. Unfortunately, you were not born into the "haves." It may not be fair, but I'm certainly necessary. You want to become a multimillionaire, right? Well, you can use my help, too. I've got a feeling, however, that you'll live richly without depending on my existence. I can already see how nearly ten years of therapy has transformed your relationship to riches.

I know I'm the last you'd want advice from, but I implore you to leap. Leap and trust the magic of a new beginning. You are well past my grip.

Sincerely,
Poverty

Write a letter from a circumstance you couldn't control.

A Letter to/from an Event in History that Impacted Me

Dear Crack Epidemic,

You came in and crashed on us, on my family.

You sat in every room and in every nook of our three-bedroom seventh floor apartment in that sixteen-story building.

You sat in my bedroom at the edge of my bed begging me for four dollars that I was saving for tithes.

You came to my classroom with me when those three roaches crawled out the radio that I brought to school to celebrate my teacher's birthday.

You sat in every crevice of the cabinets of my home in the darkness of the day so when we'd open the cabinets the roaches would come rushing out.

You sat beside me on the school bus when I was pretending I wasn't hungry because I didn't have money for lunch.

You came with me into the bathrooms in the stall where I use tissue as pads because it's what I had to do.

You single-handedly destroyed the foundation of my life—of so many lives.

I resent you and capitalism and so many other structures that were dogmatic about taking away our peace, our innocence, and our opportunities.

We were singing, "To be young, gifted, and Black" with chains surrounding us. People talk about the "devil" as a guy with thorns in his head and fire all around him. But in my mind, I picture you.

Signed,
A woman who broke the chains

Write a letter to/from an event in history that impacted you.

....
....
....
....
....
....
....
....
....
....
....
....
....
....
....
....
....
....
....
....
....
....
....
....

Write a letter from an experience in your life
you wish you could change.

Part 5: Letters to and from Feelings

what feelings
have you
suppressed, denied,
or buried?

Letters to Feelings You've Had and What They May Want to Say to You or You to Them

For me, it's grief, rage, love, and surrenderance. The peace I felt being able to hold each of them has been sobering. I feel regret for ever rejecting them, for every time I buried or subdued them. I am sorry for every time I denied them existence or tried to make them palatable to anyone. I am sorry for judging them when I met them in others and in myself. I am now able to welcome them as Rumi talked about in the poem, "Guest House."

Dear Grief,

I didn't know how much I needed to meet you. It was your insistence that made me open the door for you to enter. It is your tenderness and your quiet and your screams that made me listen to you. I was soooooo afraid of you. If I let you in, would I lose my identity? Would I lose the things I'd been holding on to as a badge? What would it cost me to know you?

Thank you for staying close. Thank you for being gentle when I needed gentleness and for being bold when I needed that, too. I am grateful you come whenever you're needed, without my having to ask and you stay as long as you know I need you to. You are never timing me, just sitting with me. You leave only when your work is done.

From,
An open and healing heart

Write a letter to a feeling you buried.

Dear Rage,

WTH! Who knew we'd been friends for so long? I had no idea we met when I was so young. I have so many questions for you as it seems you know way more about me than I do you. I thought you only befriended people who can't control themselves. I thought you were only meant for harm. I had no idea you also engage from love. Wow. I now know I can express myself without being afraid of how you might make others feel. I now know there is some of you in each of us, sometimes waiting to be met. Thank you for joining me on my healing journey. You've been such a crucial part of it. I am sorry for not seeing that sooner. I am no longer afraid of you. I see you. I thank you for expressing yourself through me, even when it's imperfect, so that I can release the things that would have otherwise stifled me.

Love,
Rageful parts of me

Write a letter to a feeling that has overwhelmed you.

Dear Pleasure,

MY GOODNESS! It took me so long to let you in because I was trying to keep out rage and grief and anger, not even realizing that you all use the same door to enter.

Thank you for staying on the other side of the door until I figured out how to unlock it to let you in. Thank you for sending pieces of you through the crevices of the door and walls and windows to dance with me. Thank you for holding space for me even when I couldn't hold it for you.

Pleasure, you've always felt like a dirty word. But I am learning that you are part of life's ecosystem. I deserve to experience you, and you me. I am worthy of the gift of pleasure, of goodness, of gentleness, of light...you bring it all.

Thank you for sticking by me even when I have rejected you.

Love,
The Embracing Version of Me

Write a letter to a feeling you're learning to embrace.

Dear Surrender,

I am yours. I belong to you.

As a daughter of the sun—the sun that meets me inside my body and rises every morning outside my window—I understand you well.

We've had a complex relationship because I was in love with control and it resented you. But you are special. You help me live with the ease I know is mine to have. You remind me to flow, to trust, to listen, to roll with it and to be where my feet are, to give in to the moment.

Thank you for being willing to develop such a beautiful relationship with me after all these years of me avoiding you. I love belonging to you. You reflect my favorite part of life.

Thank you all for all the ways you make my life fulfilling!

Love,
The Integrated Me

Write a letter to a feeling you want to reconnect to.

Dear Readers,

You've written the letters. You've probably shed a few tears and told yourself truths you may not have before. Give yourself a hug. Take a few deep breaths. You are healing. You are growing. You are on a journey. Keep going.

One of the major shifts I've experienced since writing my letters is how I relate to my parents. I used to say, "My parents were addicts." Now I say, "My parents were impacted by the crack epidemic." Both statements are true, but I carry them differently. The second statement leaves space for my parents' humanity and acknowledges the ills of addiction, poverty, and capitalism.

Another thing that shifted for me is my relationship with beauty. I realized that so many people have insecurities. So many people want to change things about who they are and compare themselves to others. So, in a world of "I wish I looked like that," I am taking photoshoots and celebrating who I am and what I look like now. I owe it to my younger self and to my future self.

I am already enough as I am. I am already beautiful as I am.

Write a Letter to Future You

What do you want to remember from this letter-writing experience?
How has this experience changed you? What is possible now that
you've gone through this process?

....
....
....
....
....
....
....
....
....
....
....
....
....
....
....
....
....
....
....
....
....
....

ABOUT MIA ROSE DUNLAP

Mia Rose Dunlap grew up on Chicago's Southside where she navigated the adversity of poverty, homelessness, and family addiction disorder. With courage and commitment, Dunlap graduated from Spelman College in Atlanta, GA, making her a first-generation high school and college graduate in her family. She later moved to New York City where she lived for a decade and earned her master's degree, became an educator, and started her business as a self-development coach and speaker. Mia Rose attributes her success to her village of angels who were her safe havens, extended time in therapy, her faith, and her ability to creatively use her imagination to manifest a life different from the one she'd known.

Mia Rose is most proud of having backpacked three months through Europe, being a three-time Cornell University retreat speaker & facilitator, and leading corporate wellness sessions across the country. She has been featured in ShoutOut Atlanta, BlackLoveTM, Voyage Atlanta, and KISH Magazine for her creative approach to storytelling and wellness. Mia Rose's web-series, "The Audacity Show," features champions who share their journeys of overcoming adversity and having the audacity to curate a life they love. The fourth season is an exclusive interview with her mother and focuses on apologies, healing, and repair. In Atlanta, Mia Rose continues to focus on group coaching, hosting creative wellness experiences, and writing. She is the author of *The Audacity to Curate a Life You Love.* Her focus in this season is informed by Parker Palmer's *Let Your Life Speak.*

www.ingramcontent.com/pod-product-compliance
Lightning Source LLC
Chambersburg PA
CBHW051222120626
46547CB00013B/1469

* 9 7 8 1 9 6 3 8 7 4 5 3 2 *